Usborne Quicklinks

To find out more about rockets and spacecraft,
go to the Usborne Quicklinks website at
www.usborne.com/quicklinks
and type in the title of this book.

Acknowledgements

Every effort has been made to trace and acknowledge ownership
of copyright. If any rights have been omitted, the publishers offer
to rectify this in any future editions following notification.
The publishers are grateful to Lockheed Martin Space Systems
Company for their permission to depict the Orion spacecraft, and to
Reaction Engines for their permission to depict the Skylon spacecraft.
With many thanks to the following organizations for their permission
to reproduce material on the following pages:

Note: the letter b indicates the inner pages of a fold-out page.

Photographs of the Moon on p1 and p10-11 © NASA/JPL
Photograph of Earth on cover, p2-3, p4-5, p12b-13b © NASA/NOAA
Photographs of Mars on p8-9 both © NASA/JPL/Cornell
Photograph of nebula on p14 © NASA, ESA and the
Hubble Heritage Team (STScI/AURA)
Photograph of Mars on p16-17 © NASA/JPL/Cornell

Series designer: Laura Wood   Series editor: Jane Chisholm
Image manipulation: John Russell

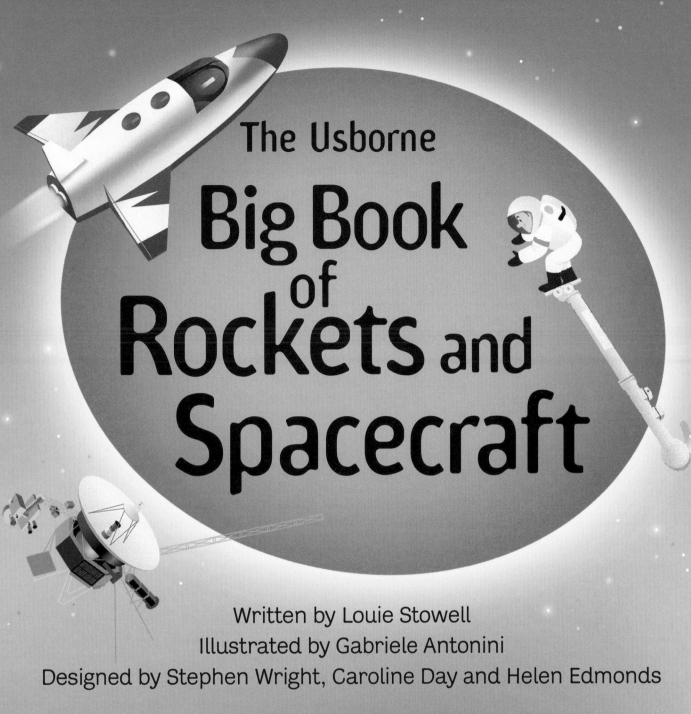

The Usborne
Big Book
of
Rockets and
Spacecraft

Written by Louie Stowell
Illustrated by Gabriele Antonini
Designed by Stephen Wright, Caroline Day and Helen Edmonds

Space experts: Gianluigi Baldesi and Stuart Atkinson

Flying in space

All spacecraft fly in space, but some stay fairly close to home, flying in circles around the Earth. This is known as orbiting. Earth itself orbits the Sun, along with seven other planets. Some spacecraft fly far into space to visit these planets, or even land on them.

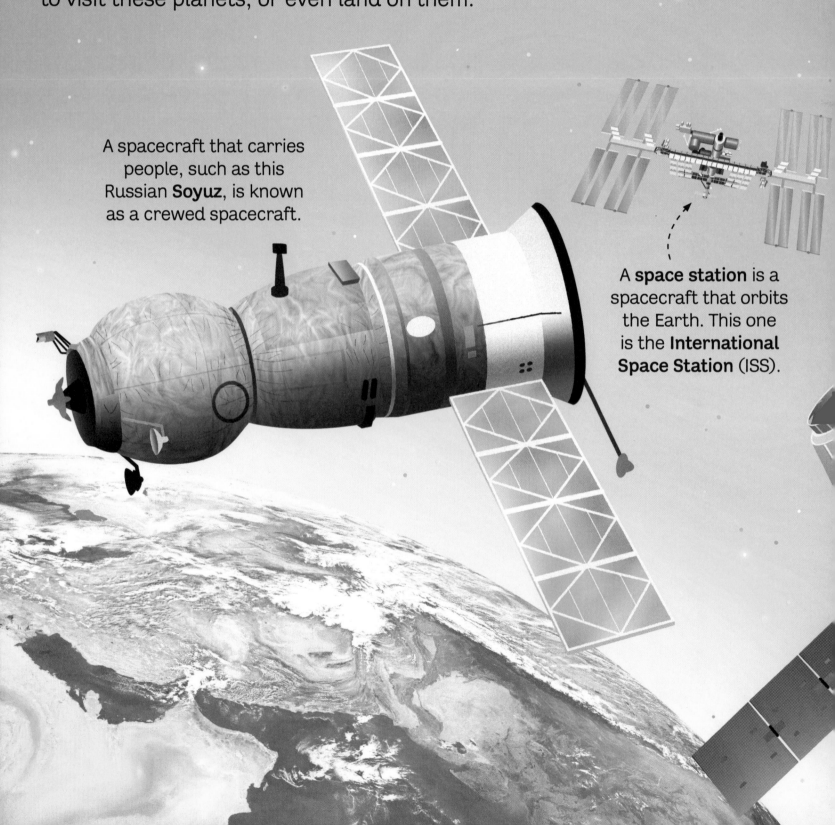

A spacecraft that carries people, such as this Russian **Soyuz**, is known as a crewed spacecraft.

A **space station** is a spacecraft that orbits the Earth. This one is the **International Space Station** (ISS).

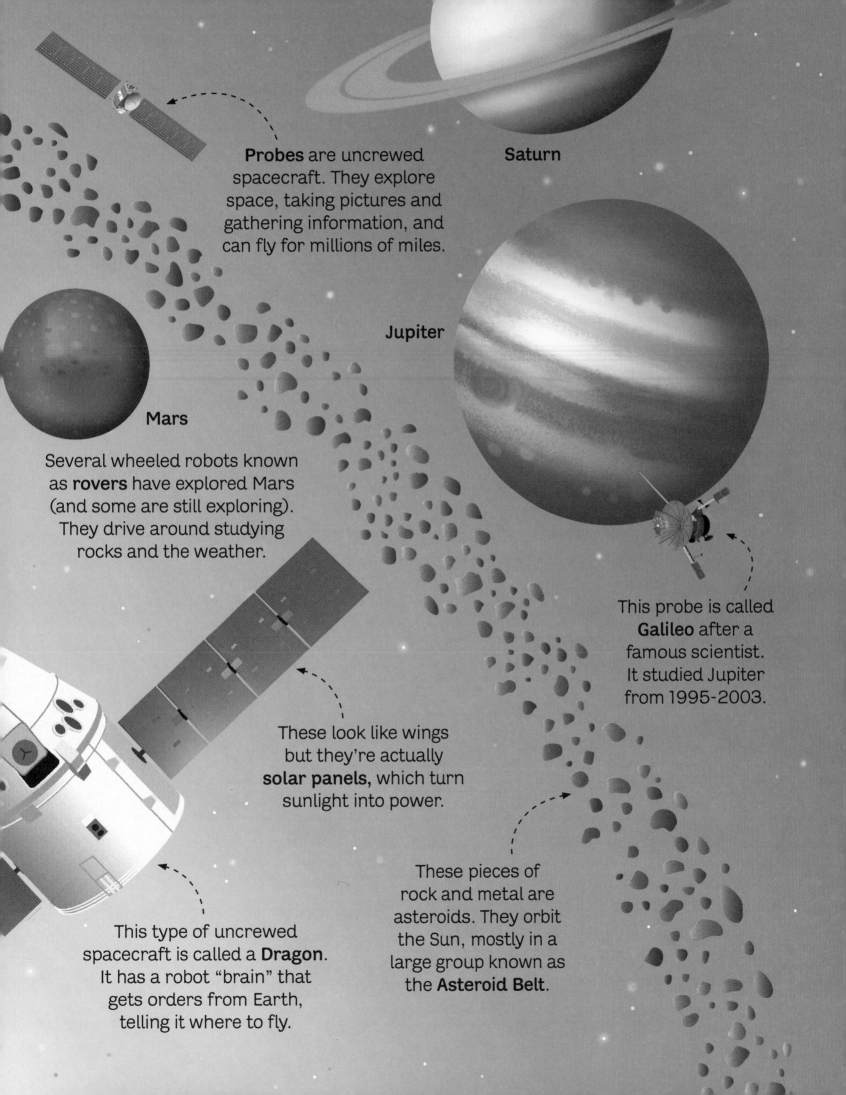

Saturn

Probes are uncrewed spacecraft. They explore space, taking pictures and gathering information, and can fly for millions of miles.

Jupiter

Mars

Several wheeled robots known as **rovers** have explored Mars (and some are still exploring). They drive around studying rocks and the weather.

This probe is called **Galileo** after a famous scientist. It studied Jupiter from 1995-2003.

These look like wings but they're actually **solar panels,** which turn sunlight into power.

These pieces of rock and metal are asteroids. They orbit the Sun, mostly in a large group known as the **Asteroid Belt**.

This type of uncrewed spacecraft is called a **Dragon**. It has a robot "brain" that gets orders from Earth, telling it where to fly.

Liftoff

To get into space, rockets first have to fight against gravity. Gravity is the "pull" that stops people and things on Earth from floating away into space.

Rockets, or launch vehicles, are made up of lots of rocket engines, also known as **stages**. Each stage falls off after firing.

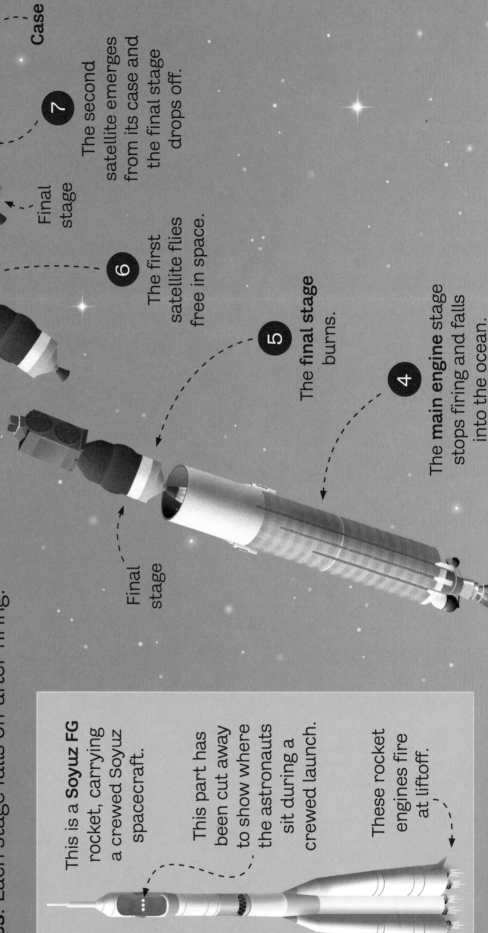

First satellite

Solar panels

First satellite

Final stage

8 Eventually, both satellites stretch out their solar panels, which will power them as they fly in orbit around Earth.

Case

7 The second satellite emerges from its case and the final stage drops off.

Final stage

6 The first satellite flies free in space.

5 The final **stage** burns.

4 The **main engine** stage stops firing and falls into the ocean.

This is a **Soyuz FG** rocket, carrying a crewed Soyuz spacecraft.

This part has been cut away to show where the astronauts sit during a crewed launch.

These rocket engines fire at liftoff.

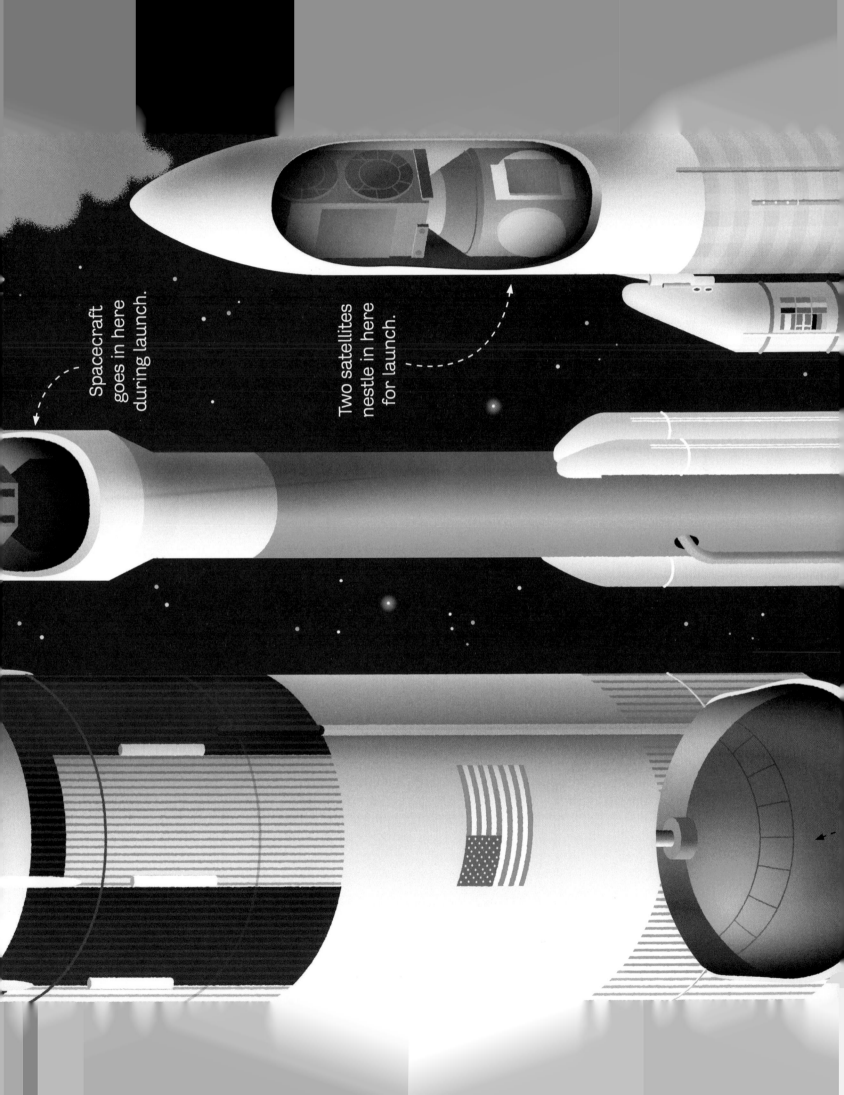

Spacecraft goes in here during launch.

Two satellites nestle in here for launch.

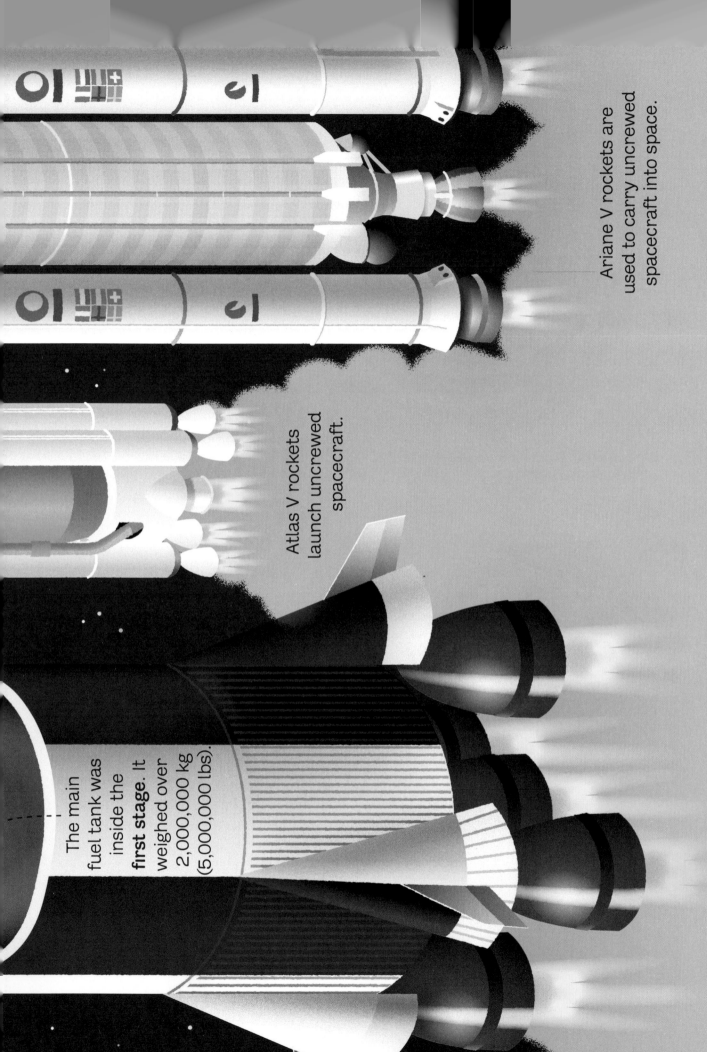

Ariane V rockets are used to carry uncrewed spacecraft into space.

Atlas V rockets launch uncrewed spacecraft.

The main fuel tank was inside the **first stage**. It weighed over 2,000,000 kg (5,000,000 lbs).

Saturn V rockets were used between 1967 and 1973. In 1969, a Saturn V launched three astronauts on the first mission to the Moon. Before it launched, the rocket stood 110 m (363 ft) tall. That's taller than the Big Ben tower in London.

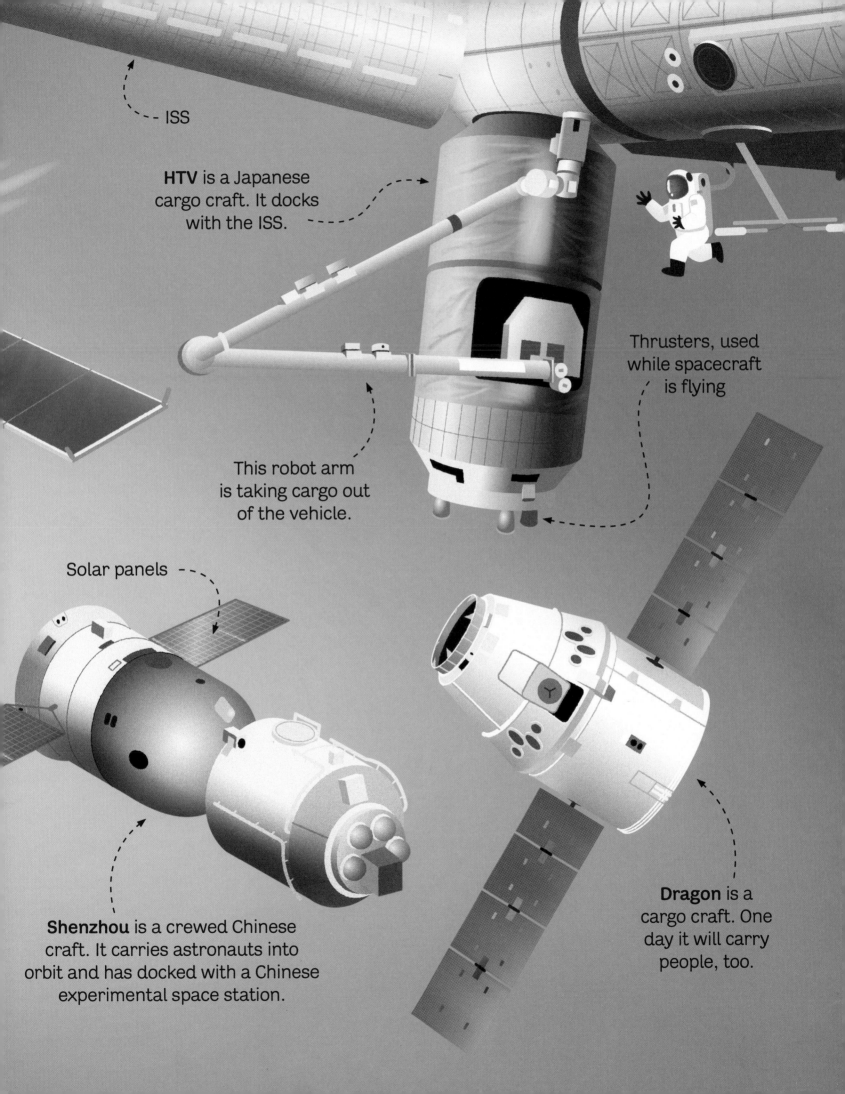

ISS

HTV is a Japanese cargo craft. It docks with the ISS.

Thrusters, used while spacecraft is flying

This robot arm is taking cargo out of the vehicle.

Solar panels

Shenzhou is a crewed Chinese craft. It carries astronauts into orbit and has docked with a Chinese experimental space station.

Dragon is a cargo craft. One day it will carry people, too.

Robot explorers

Sending humans far into space is dangerous and expensive, so uncrewed spacecraft are used for longer missions. Such as...

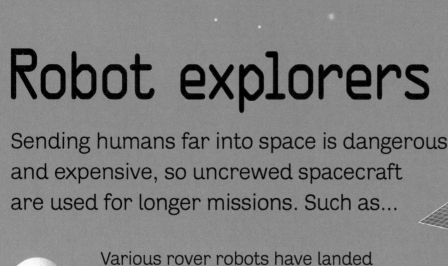

Various rover robots have landed on Mars. The latest is **Curiosity**, which landed in 2012.

Mars Orbital Mission (MOM) was launched in November 2013. It's orbiting Mars.

1
A parachute opened to slow the craft holding Curiosity.

2
Curiosity was lowered out of the craft and thrusters slowed it down more.

Curiosity

Antenna receives instructions about where to drive.

A laser turns parts of rocks into a mist that is analyzed to see what the rock is made from.

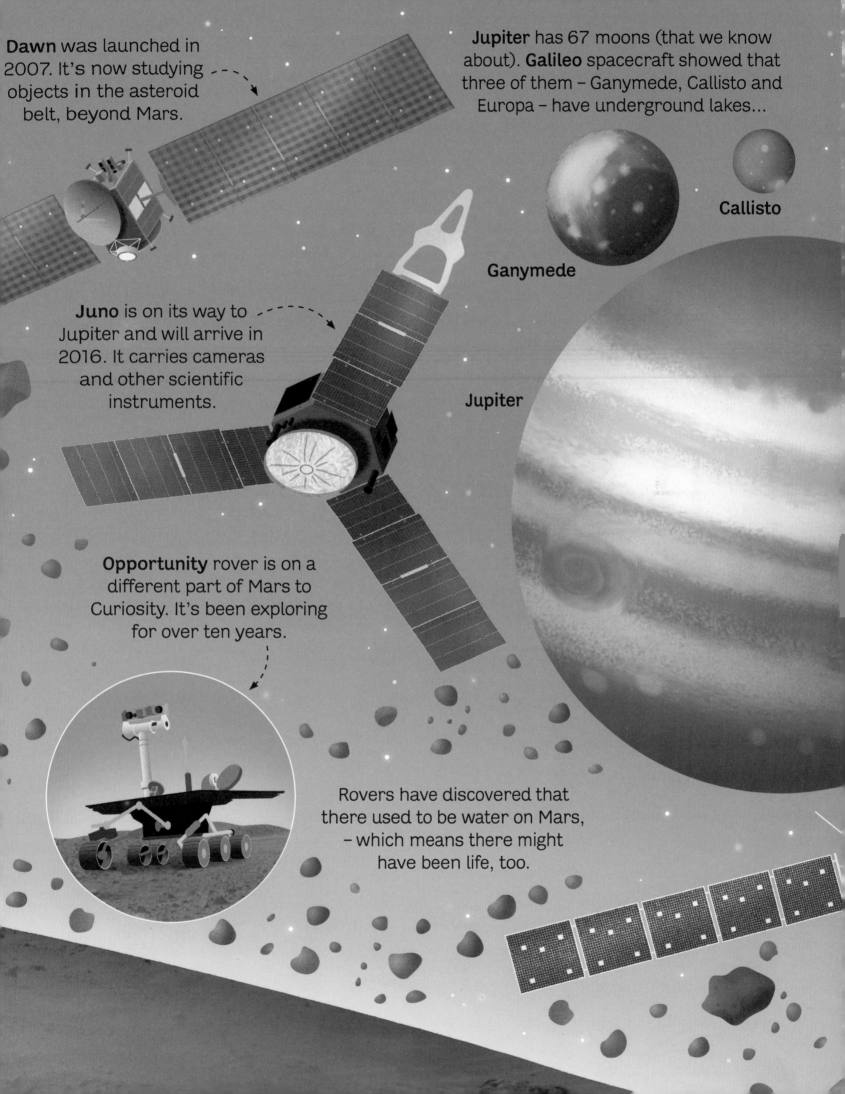

Dawn was launched in 2007. It's now studying objects in the asteroid belt, beyond Mars.

Jupiter has 67 moons (that we know about). **Galileo** spacecraft showed that three of them – Ganymede, Callisto and Europa – have underground lakes...

Ganymede

Callisto

Juno is on its way to Jupiter and will arrive in 2016. It carries cameras and other scientific instruments.

Jupiter

Opportunity rover is on a different part of Mars to Curiosity. It's been exploring for over ten years.

Rovers have discovered that there used to be water on Mars, – which means there might have been life, too.

The Space Race

In the 1950s, a "Space Race" began between the governments of the United States of America and the Soviet Union — an old name for Russia and surrounding countries.

During the Second World War, the Germans built an exploding rocket called the **V-2**. Scientists realized the technology could be used to explore space.

In 1957, Soviet craft **Sputnik** became the first spacecraft to orbit Earth.

Later in 1957, a dog called Laika was the first animal to orbit Earth.

In 1961, Soviet spacecraft **Vostok 1** carried Yuri Gagarin, the first human in space.

The Soviet Union sent robotic **Luna** probes to the Moon, starting in 1959.

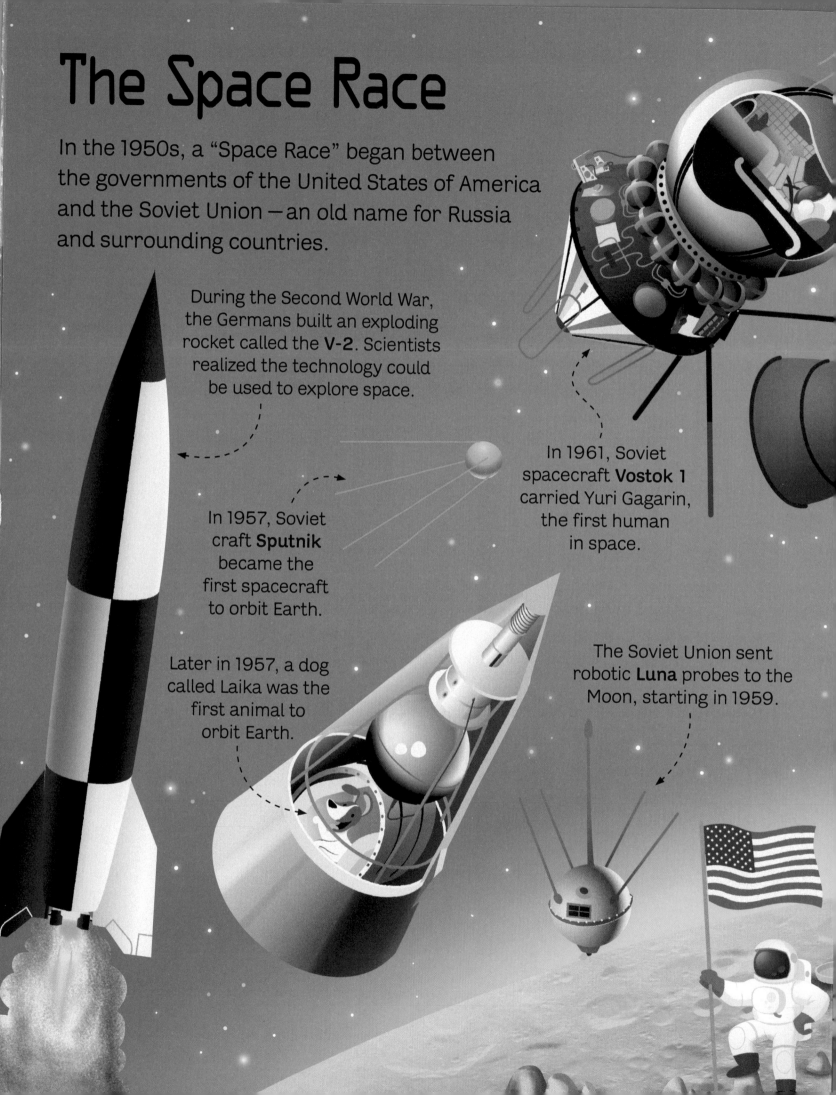

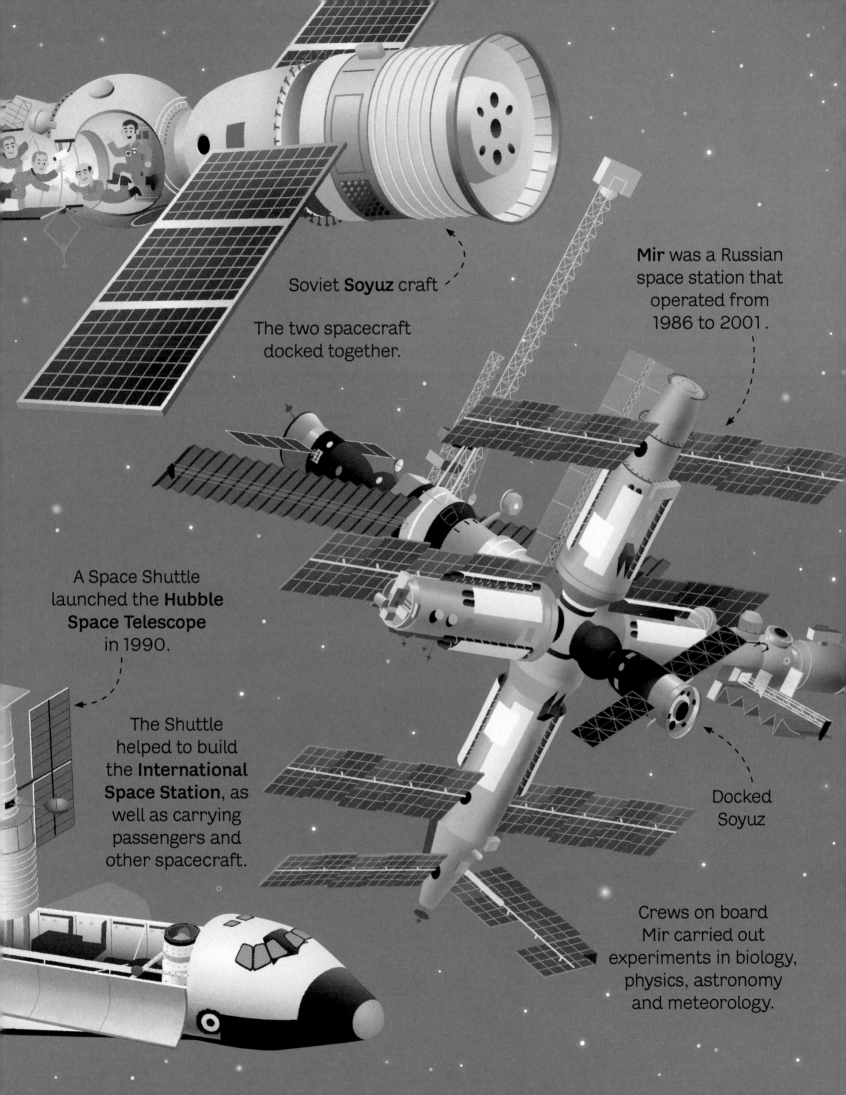

Soviet **Soyuz** craft

The two spacecraft docked together.

Mir was a Russian space station that operated from 1986 to 2001.

A Space Shuttle launched the **Hubble Space Telescope** in 1990.

The Shuttle helped to build the **International Space Station**, as well as carrying passengers and other spacecraft.

Docked Soyuz

Crews on board Mir carried out experiments in biology, physics, astronomy and meteorology.

Space stations

Astronauts can live on board space stations for months at a time, doing scientific experiments. In the past, space stations were even used to spy on enemy countries.

Salyut 7 was a Soviet space station in orbit from 1982-91.

Soyuz spacecraft docked with Salyut 7

Almaz was a top-secret Soviet space station used for spying.

Skylab was the first US space station, launched as a space laboratory in 1973.

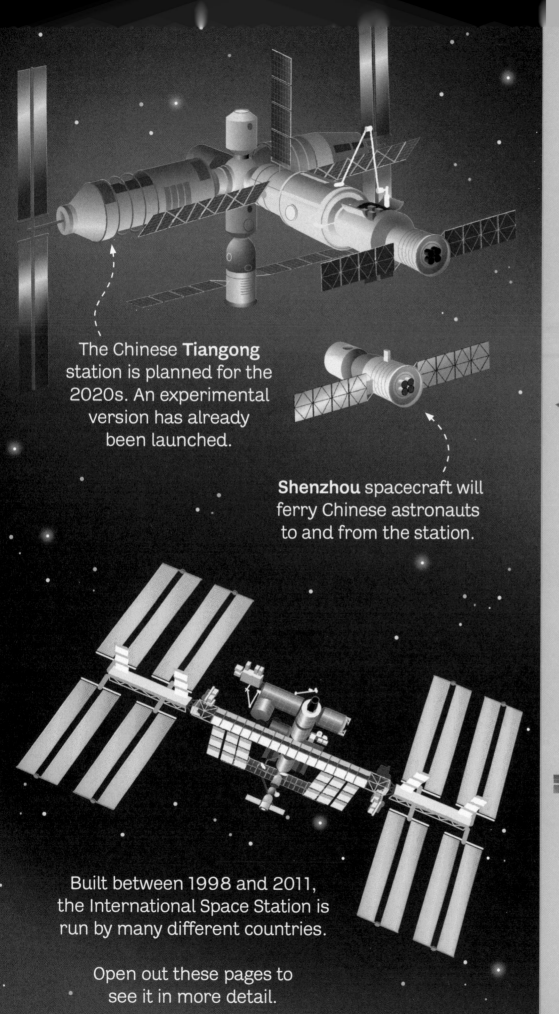

The Chinese **Tiangong** station is planned for the 2020s. An experimental version has already been launched.

Shenzhou spacecraft will ferry Chinese astronauts to and from the station.

Built between 1998 and 2011, the International Space Station is run by many different countries.

Open out these pages to see it in more detail.

Modern space stations are built in space.

Each module is flown up separately.

Each new module docks with an earlier module, until the station is complete.

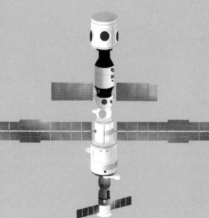

The ISS is made up of 14 modules, as well as solar panels and other outside parts.

Eyes in the sky

Satellites orbit Earth and are used to beam messages from one country to another, or to study our planet. Spacecraft that gather information about outer space are called space telescopes or space observatories.

Hubble takes pictures of beautiful clouds of space dust and other spectacular sights.

Hubble is a space telescope that's been taking photographs for over 25 years.

Herschel flew from 2009 to 2013. It used a type of light called infrared to study space.

When Hubble needed repairs, a Space Shuttle "caught" it using a robot arm. Then astronauts in space suits went outside to do the repairs.

Herschel was named after a brother and sister team of astronomers from the 1700s.

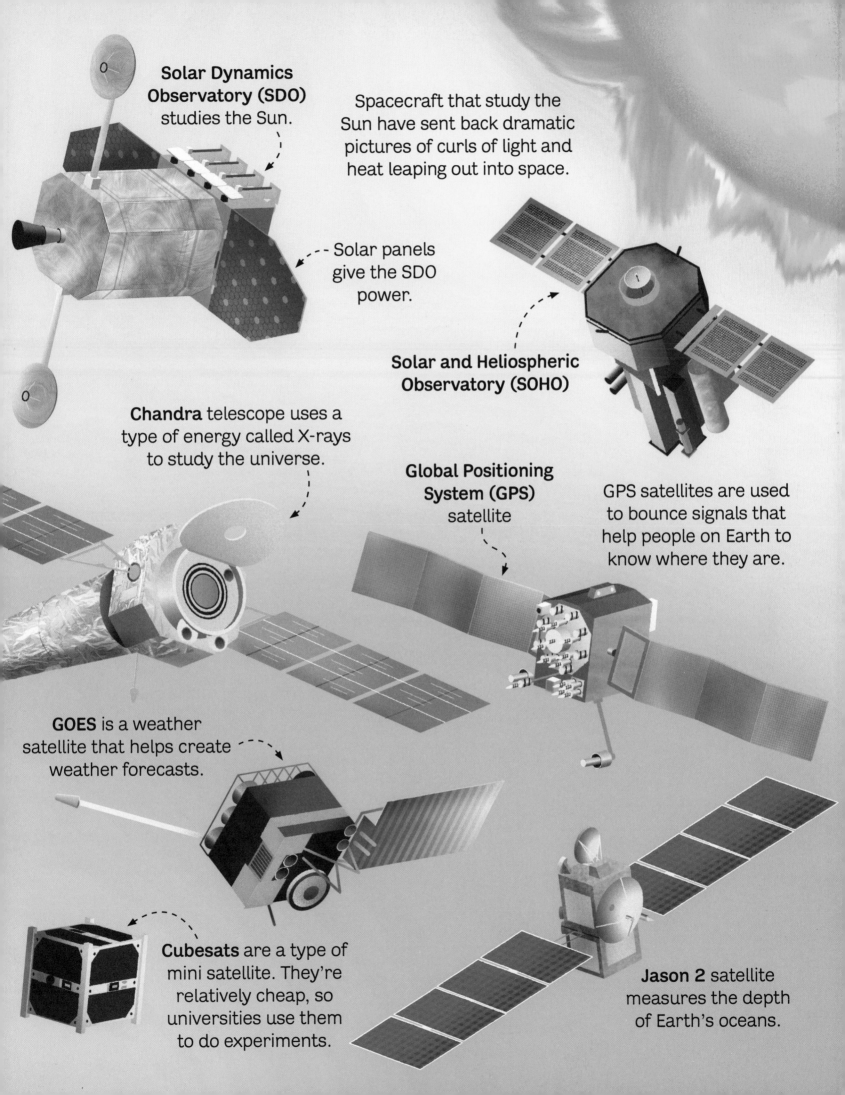

Solar Dynamics Observatory (SDO) studies the Sun.

Spacecraft that study the Sun have sent back dramatic pictures of curls of light and heat leaping out into space.

Solar panels give the SDO power.

Solar and Heliospheric Observatory (SOHO)

Chandra telescope uses a type of energy called X-rays to study the universe.

Global Positioning System (GPS) satellite

GPS satellites are used to bounce signals that help people on Earth to know where they are.

GOES is a weather satellite that helps create weather forecasts.

Cubesats are a type of mini satellite. They're relatively cheap, so universities use them to do experiments.

Jason 2 satellite measures the depth of Earth's oceans.

The future

Here are some designs for spacecraft of the future. Some are planned to fly soon. Others are still twinkles in the eyes of scientists.

Satellite being launched

This is the **Orion** spacecraft. It's designed to carry humans deep into space. It has already been built and is being tested.

Skylon is a planned, uncrewed spacecraft, which will launch using built-in, air-breathing rocket engines.

This is one of a few designs for robot spacecraft whose job is to clear away broken spaceships.

Broken spacecraft

The pilot would sit at the front, with passengers behind.

In the next few years, tourists (with a lot of money) should be able to take short flights up into space on crafts like this.

Fuel goes here.

Engines

A craft like this wouldn't need a launch vehicle, as it has rocket engines built into the main spacecraft.

A wheel-shaped spinning space station could create artificial gravity, allowing astronauts to live more as they do on Earth. Gravity is good for your bones, so it would make astronauts healthier, too.

Some scientists have suggested it might be possible to build ships that can go faster than light —299,792km (186,282 miles) per second! That would make it possible to explore distant planets.

One day people might build bases on other planets or moons. Scientists could live and work there. Here's what a Mars base might look like.

Mars buggies to carry people between their habitation domes. They could also be used to do work such as mining.

Greenhouse for growing food

People would have to live in sealed domes as you can't breathe outside on Mars, and it's very cold.

Spacesuits for working outside

Solar panels

Robot rovers to help scientists do their work.